ANTOINE GRIEZMANN
The Kid Who Never Gave Up

A special thank you to Yonatan, Yaron and Guy Ginsberg.

Cover photos ©   AP Photo/Joan Monfort

Cover design and inside page layout: Lazar Kackarovski

Proof editor: Marc Murphy-Robinson

Library of Congress Cataloging-in-Publication data available.

ISBN: 978-1-938591-76-1

eBook ISBN: 978-1-938591-77-8

Published by Sole Books, Beverly Hills, California.

Printed in the United States of America

First edition November 2019

www.solebooks.com

Antoine Griezmann

THE KID WHO NEVER GAVE UP

Michael Part
and
Steve Berg

Read more in the Soccer Stars Series:

www.solebooks.com

CHAPTER 1

Too Small, Again

The mood was somber in the Griezmann family home. Thirteen-year-old Antoine sat across from his dad, Alain, at the kitchen table. His mom, Isabelle, was at the counter, slicing an apple pie. She knew that something sweet would relax everyone. Alain stared blankly, thinking hard. From the back of the house, Antoine could hear his brother Theo and his sister Maud laughing. He hadn't broken the news to them yet.

"They told me I'm too small," Antoine said. "Again." He was still upset. *It's not my fault*, he thought. *Someday, it won't matter.* He just hoped it wouldn't be too late.

"I'll write the FC Metz coaches a letter," Alain said angrily. "Tell them exactly what I think about all this."

"I don't want to go to any more tryouts," Antoine said. "They're a waste of time." He felt the tears welling up. He looked out through the kitchen window. In the community center basketball court, adjacent to their home, a bunch of kids was having a pickup soccer game. That's where he wanted to be. Especially today. He wanted to take his ball and run out. That's where he'd always wanted to be, ever since he learned how to walk: a ball glued to his feet.

"I know how it feels," his mom said "You certainly deserve a break from trying to get onto a team. Eat the pie dear, it will make you feel better." She placed a nice wide slice in front of him.

"Thank you, Mom," Antoine said.

"I even sent them an x-ray of your wrist, showing that it's nothing permanent, that your growth is just a year behind your age group, that's all," his dad said. "I don't get it. Don't they understand that you are going to grow and get stronger in a year or two?"

"The recruiter said I was great," Antoine said in a trembling voice.

His dad, who was his coach, nodded in agreement. "It was a spectacular performance," he said in a softer voice. "The team was at its best. And so were you."

A couple of weeks earlier, a recruiter for FC Metz had come down to Macon, where the Griezmanns lived, to watch the local under-13s play. Macon, a small city in the center east of France, not far from Lyon, didn't have a notable football club, but the recruiter had been told that the U-13 team was packed with talent.

This was his job: going to local youth games and looking for kids who showed a spark. Discovering future stars with the hope that, one day, they'd grow up to become great.

When he took his seat in the stands, close to the halfway line, he hoped that the match against FC Sens would be worth the trip. During the game, he scribbled notes in a small notepad. The man near him looked sideways, trying to figure out what he was writing. The recruiter just smiled and kept writing. He didn't think the other fellow could decipher his notes.

Macon demolished the guests and the recruiter couldn't take his eyes off the small blond kid. He looked younger than everyone else on the pitch but made the fans cheer wildly for him, with four assists and one amazing goal. The kid got the ball outside the 18-yard box. He intercepted it with his chest, turned around and, before the ball hit the ground, kicked it hard into the left corner above the helpless goalkeeper.

The recruiter clapped and cheered along with the fans. It was his job to watch hundreds of games each year. And he knew this kid was special.

He scribbled *BD*! then turned to a man who sat next to him.

"Who's the little blond devil?" he asked. That explained the cryptic *BD*! he had just written.

"Griezmann. Antoine. Amazing, isn't he?" the man asked, and the recruiter sensed there was pride in how he said it. "This kid and the ball," he continued, "You can't separate them. He loves the game more than anything."

"It shows," said the recruiter. "He's good."

"His dad is the coach," said the man and pointed to Alain who stood on the sideline, yelling instructions to his players.

Good tip, the recruiter thought.

"Thanks," he said to the man.

After the game, he went down to the pitch and introduced himself to the *blond devil's* father. Out on the field, Antoine celebrated the victory with his teammates and, at first, didn't see the man. Even when he finally noticed him, it didn't register. *Just another one*, he thought, looking for talent, talking to his dad about him and his friends. He couldn't care less.

The recruiter later emailed his report to the youth program managers back in Metz. "Antoine Griezmann, age 13. Very good game vision. Great left foot. Midfielder. Good passer. Leader of the team. Assists and scores. Good ball control. A bit small for his age. Invite him to a tryout. Urgent!"

One Friday afternoon, Alain and Antoine headed to Metz. The city was situated in Lorraine in northeastern France, a three-hour drive from Macon. Antoine was excited. And although he had come home empty-handed from his last five tryouts, he quickly let go of the disappointment. And, as his dad and he made their way up north, he felt confident he'd make it this time. The recruiter had told his dad that he stood out. And he didn't mind that he was small, which was a good sign.

When they arrived at the training facility everyone was nice to them. The two coaches, Sebastian and Olivier, monitored him. They thought he was good, but they weren't 100% sure because of his size. After training, they told Alain that they wanted to see Antoine play in a match. They had a friendly with a German team coming up. Alain thought it was a good idea. He was convinced his son would shine.

Antoine proved his father right. He was the best player on the pitch. He helped in defense. He was there for many assists. His passes were immaculate. He was everywhere. It seemed at times that Antoine Griezmann was the only player on the pitch.

"How'd I do?" Antoine asked his dad after the game.

"Perfect," Alain said.

The coaches seemed to agree. A few days later when Antoine came back from school, he saw his dad beaming.

"They want you!" he announced.

"Yes!" Antoine yelled.

FC Metz offered to sign Antoine to their academy where he'd live, study, and train during the week. On weekends, he'd go back home and train with Macon.

Isabelle wasn't sure about her son being away at first. But Antoine was so excited that she agreed. Alain called the Metz coaches and said, "We want to do it."

They told him it would take a few more days to finish the paperwork.

A week later there was another phone call.

Alain's face was flushed with anger when he hung up the phone. He first broke the news to Isabelle. Then he went outside. He knew exactly where Antoine was. He could hear the ball hammering against the garage door. Antoine was kicking a ball with his left foot. The ball bounced back only to meet his foot and go back to the painted blue door, covered with marks from years of kicking.

Antoine noticed his dad. He stopped at once.

"Is Mom angry?" he asked. He knew the noise could make her unhappy sometimes, especially when he practiced for a long time.

"No, no, nothing like that," his dad said. "I just wanted to talk to you for a moment."

Antoine sensed his hesitation. "What about?"

"Metz."

"You got the papers?"

"No son. No papers." Alain felt a knot in his throat. "There's not going to be any papers. They changed their minds."

Antoine studied his father for a long moment. "Why?" He looked him in the eye.

"They think you are…"

"Too small?"

His dad nodded.

Antoine felt the world crashing in on him. He started to cry. Alain hugged him.

"Let's go inside. See what we can do," he said.

Dinner was over. Theo and Maud were told about Metz. The mood grew even grimmer.

"What are you going to put in the letter to Metz?" Isabelle asked her husband.

"I'm going to tell them that one day they are going to regret giving up on Antoine Griezmann."

"One day," Isabelle said, "there'll come a team that will take you because of your qualities as a player, not because of your physique."

"Your mother's right," his dad said. "But I'm still writing the letter."

Ten minutes later, Antoine was on the court. The neighborhood kids greeted him. Everyone knew him. Everyone wanted him on their side. He joined the game and scored a quick goal. From the kitchen window, his mom watched him, his blond hair bouncing around as he dribbled his way to the goal. He was smiling again. She knew why. When the ball was at his feet, everything was right with his world.

CHAPTER 2

The Drawing

Antoine cut small pieces from his rubber eraser and lined them up on his desk like players before a game. Jean-Baptiste, his best friend since they were little kids, knew what was coming. He tried to listen to Catherine, their teacher, who was talking about the French revolution. Antoine liked the sound of his teacher's voice, but he wasn't really listening. His journal was opened wide and he was putting the finishing touches to a drawing.

The teacher's husband was the head of their local football club. Antoine liked her, but he was bored. He didn't care much about school. What he really liked was recess and playing outside in the schoolyard. He touched the ball that was idle under his desk. The ball went with him everywhere. He had a dozen in his house, but this one was the one he loved best. It was scratched and worn out, but he didn't care. He felt a bond with his ball. Two minutes left to recess. It was time for some fun.

Catherine turned around and wrote something on the board. Antoine picked up a couple of rubber pieces and threw them in fast succession toward two girls who were sitting in the front row. The rubber pieces hit them simultaneously on both their backs. It was beautiful. And Jean-Baptiste was impressed because the two girls were seated at opposite corners of the room. It took great skill to hit his targets so swiftly and yet accurately. Jean-Baptiste gave his friend the thumbs up. Antoine threw two more rubber balls. This time he hit his other best friend, Martin, in his face.

Martin turned his head and faked a scowl. He knew the drill. He had his own rubber projectile ready.

Students giggled when Martin threw the tiny rubber ball at Antoine, who ducked expertly. Ms. Catherine turned around to face the class. All motion among the students froze in time. Something was up. She saw Martin's upraised hand, hanging in the air. Antoine, on the other hand, was nowhere to be seen. She sensed immediately what had been going on behind her back.

Jean-Baptiste looked over to the window, trying desperately to hold back his laughter. Antoine sat stock still with a blank stare. The bell rang. Saved again. He smiled and let his breath out.

The students got up to leave. Ms. Catherine stopped Antoine, ball already tucked under his arm, on his way out the door. "Antoine," she said calmly. "May I have a word with you?

"Yes madam," he said. Even if he sensed trouble, you couldn't see it in his expression. He ran his fingers through his wavy blond hair and shot her one of his best grins.

"You didn't turn in your last assignment," she said.

He looked at her and she realized he had no idea what assignment that could have been.

"Yesterday, I had a chat with your mom," his teacher said. "She told me that whenever she asks you about your homework, you tell her you don't have any."

He looked embarrassed. "Well," he said, "That's not 100% untrue. Occasionally we don't."

The teacher smiled. "You're a bright kid. You are going to have to do more. You're going to have to try harder, Antoine."

Antoine sucked in a nervous breath. "I will," he said, meaning it for the moment.

She stared him down and knew there was only one thing he wanted to do and studying or homework wasn't it. He wanted to play. So, she made him wait.

She checked her watch after ten seconds.

"You may go now," she finally said.

It felt like an eternity to Antoine. He thanked her and dashed out of the classroom. He ran down the spiral staircase of Georges Brassens primary school, bobbed-and-weaved through other students, with only one thing in mind. He ran out of the two-story building and out onto the schoolyard and concrete playground where a court was marked-off with two small goals and one basketball hoop. A game was already in progress. "What took you so long?" Jean-Baptiste yelled. Antoine left his ball on the sideline and joined the game. "Teacher wanted to know why I haven't been doing my homework," he said. "But I think she already knows why." He looked over at the classroom and Jean-Baptiste followed his gaze. Their teacher was out on the porch, arms crossed, watching them play. Antoine waved. She waved back, then went back inside.

In a way, Antoine was right. His teacher knew he had the best grades in PE – swimming, basketball, and soccer. Unfortunately, he barely did the minimum when it came to all his other classes.

After school, Antoine walked down Rue de Normandie, his backpack on his back, his ball under his arm. Home was just a short jog down the road. Most of the five-story buildings in the Les Gautriats neighborhood were surrounded by pine trees and green grass. It was perfect for a pickup game. Antoine's eyes were wandering around, looking to see if any kids were playing. He was happy to join any game at any time. But he was hungry and soon entered his home and looked for something to eat. His mom worked as a cleaning lady at the local hospital and wasn't home. Dad was nearby at the community center. His brother and sister were at school. He grabbed an apple and went to his room. He looked at a huge David Beckham poster that was hanging on the wall. Becks smiled at him in approval.

He took out the journal from his backpack and looked at the drawing. It was of him, standing on a soccer pitch. In the background, he drew the goal and the stands with faces of cheering fans. He drew a man standing beside him with a mike. The mike had the Canal+ logo of French TV. He liked the drawing, and he sat on his bed and started to write.

TV Journalist: Mister Griezmann, that was a beautiful goal you scored in the last minute. How does it feel?

Antoine: It feels great. I'm glad I helped my team win the game. Playing for France was always my biggest dream.

Journalist: When was the first time you thought about being a professional player?

Antoine: I think I was two years old. At least, that's what they tell me. My granny says that when we went to visit her, I used to go out with my ball and look for kids I could play with. I was three and I already had a half dozen balls of my own. They say that the ball was glued to my feet. That is totally true. I slept with it.

Antoine smiled while he was writing the imaginary interview. In his mind, he was confident it would happen one day. There was no way it wouldn't. When he was done writing, he left his journal on the bed, grabbed his ball, and went outside, straight to the blue door, and did keepy uppies for twenty minutes. Then he started hitting the ball with his left foot, again and again, over and over.

His dad had told him that, to be a great player, you first should acquire superb ball control. Then, you must understand your role on the team and how to communicate with your teammates. How and when to make the right pass. And how to score. He loved dribbling, but he also loved to assist. He understood the nature of the game. Even the biggest stars relied on their teammates.

He saw his mom walking toward their home. She looked tired. He stopped kicking the ball against the blue door.

"Hello, Mom," he said. "How was your day?"

"The same," she said. "How's school?"

"Good," he said.

"Homework?"

"No homework," he said, and then remembered in a flash what Ms. Catherine told him.

"Actually, I had a talk with your teacher the other day at the market," his mom said. "She said that she gives plenty of homework."

He felt trapped.

"So, do you have homework or not?"

"Well, I – I think I might have some this time, now that you mention it," he said.

She gave him a look. "You should work harder Antoine. The world doesn't revolve around soccer."

He shrugged and thought, *actually, my world does revolve around soccer.*

"I'll try. Promise," he said.

"Come in," his mom said. "I'll make you something to eat."

CHAPTER 3

Beginners

The next day, as Antoine was on his way to school, his mom came running after him.

"Aren't you forgetting something?" she asked. He studied her for a moment. Was she furious? Or trying to hold back a laugh?

"No, what?" he asked, confused. He had the ball tucked under his arm.

"Your backpack." She held it out and he sheepishly took it from her outstretched arm. "You can't show up at school with just a ball, can you?"

He managed a smile. "I guess not," he muttered, but it wasn't such a bad idea, he thought.

"Thanks, Mom," he said.

At school, time moved slowly between classes. At the end of recess, after a great pickup game, he ran into the bathroom, washed his hands, and kicked the ball against one of the stall doors. The ball bounced back nicely, and he kicked it against another door. It was a fun game of keeping control of the ball while moving from one stall door to the next. The bell rang, but he couldn't stop now, he was totally absorbed in the game.

In class, Ms. Catherine looked at the vacant chair in the back of the class.

"Jean-Baptiste, where is Antoine?" she asked.

Jean-Baptiste made a face as if he was thinking really hard, stalling for time. That's when they started hearing a faint thumping, as if someone down the hall was hitting something against a wall.

"I think I know where he might be," he said, blushing. "Want me to go get him?"

The teacher raised an eyebrow. "Please do," she said.

Jean-Baptiste jumped to his feet and rushed out and skidded to a stop in the hall. There was the headmaster, Mr. Cornaton, standing outside the bathroom, a few doors down, arms folded across his chest, sneering.

"You in there!" he yelled, and it echoed down the corridor. Ms. Catherine stuck her head out the door of her classroom and her eyes grew as big as saucers when she saw the headmaster.

"You in there!" the headmaster shouted. "Stop that incessant racket now!"

At this point, the whole class piled out into the corridor to see what was going on and other doors at both ends of the hall swung open as students filed out to see what the ruckus was.

Meanwhile, in the bathroom, Antoine was totally absorbed in kicking the ball against the doors and counting. Twenty kicks without letting the ball hit the tile floor.

The headmaster whipped the bathroom door open and yelled again, "ENOUGH!"

Antoine freaked-out and let the ball drop and it rolled straight over to the headmaster standing in the doorway. He bent down and picked it up.

"Griezmann," he muttered. It was like an animal growl. "What do you think you are doing?"

Antoine felt sweat bead upon his forehead and drip down his nose. "P-practicing, sir," he said.

"You should be in class," said the headmaster, trying to restore his cool. He lived across from the pitch where Antoine and his friends spent hours playing after school. Sometimes, the sound of the ball hitting the garage door for hours on end was so annoying he wore earplugs in his own home!

"You should be practicing math," the headmaster said. The corridor was filled with students and teachers, most of them able to stifle their laughter. "Everyone please return to class," the headmaster ordered. He turned to Ms. Catherine and said, "Your student was here using school property – the bathroom – as a soccer pitch. He's all yours." He spun on his heel and marched down the corridor and out the door.

Ms. Catherine turned to Antoine and smiled. "Now what?"

"I'm sorry, ma'am, I got so wrapped up in my practice that I didn't hear the bell." He was truly embarrassed.

She jerked her head toward the classroom door. "Please come to class. We have wasted too much time already." At least he told the truth, she thought.

Antoine picked up his ball and followed her, Jean-Baptiste, and the rest of the students back into class. Everyone applauded when he took his seat. "Knock it off!" Ms. Catherine shouted over the classroom noise, then turned to Antoine. "I have an assignment for you," she said.

"Yes, ma'am," he said. He was ready to face the music.

"I'd like you to write an essay about your soccer ball," she said.

The entire class erupted in laughter. The teacher knew why they laughed but what she wanted from him was far from funny.

Antoine, on the other hand, was surprised and grateful. An essay about his favorite subject. It was perfect, he thought. "Yes, ma'am!" he exclaimed.

Later, at home in his room, he looked at old pictures. Here was one when he was three years old, holding a ball his grandma had given him. She lived on the other side of town and had come all the way over to present him with it.

Here was another one with one of his best friends, Andre, playing outside his home. He was four.

He opened his journal, took a deep breath of fresh air, and began to write.

When he was five and a half, he had joined his dad every Wednesday at two pm for a short drive to the pitch where the youth teams of UF Mayonnaise practiced. Dad was the coach and Antoine watched, always working the ball at the sidelines.

It was Bruno, the head coach of the team, who spotted Antoine on the sideline, practicing keepy uppies. He talked to the other coach, David, about an idea he had about Antoine. "Why not?" David said. Bruno went over and had a chat with Alain Griezmann.

"How old is Antoine?" Bruno asked Alain, who was busy coaching another squad

"Five and a half. Why?"

"I can't wait for him to come play for us," Bruno said. "He's a natural."

"Next season," Alain said. He was proud of his son, but he wanted him to grow some more before joining the team.

"Hold on," Bruno said. "Okay, you don't want him to play yet, but can we have him for practice?"

Alain smiled. He thought that was an excellent idea. He was happy it came from Bruno.

"I'll let you give him the good news," Alain said.

Bruno looked over to where Antoine was playing, nodded, and walked over. "Hello Antoine," he said. "Would you like to join our practice?"

Antoine stopped at once. He opened his eyes in wonder. "Really? But I'm only five and a half."

"You won't be playing for us on the team, not yet. But we would love for you to just practice with the team until you grow a bit older."

"And then I can join the team?" Antoine asked.

"Absolutely," Bruno replied.

Antoine jumped up and down, waving his arms. "Yes, yes, yes!" he shouted. Alain watched from a distance and laughed. His kid loved soccer more than anything, and he was grateful to Bruno.

Antoine ran in and joined the other kids who were in the middle of passing practice. He was one of them now. It felt great. Bruno watched, amused at how the little kid fit in with the team almost immediately. They had a pickup game and the little one scored a goal and made two assists. Everyone cheered.

Later, Antoine told his dad it was the best day of his life.

Antoine never missed a practice and always cheered his team from the bench.

One day, the team went to an away game and were losing one-zero with ten minutes left on the clock.

"Maybe we should bring Antoine in," David said.

Antoine was on the bench, cheering his teammates.

"Why not?" Bruno agreed.

He went to the bench. "We want you in," he told Antoine.

"Really!?"

Bruno saw the surprise and then the joy spread on the little boy's face.

"Get ready," Bruno told him. Before the boy went in, he said, "We need a goal."

"I think we need two," Antoine said. He was almost six and, even at that tender age, he wouldn't settle for a tie.

He went in. His first goal came two minutes later, from a run he made from midfield to the box dribbling with the ball glued to his feet. He was unstoppable. He didn't run into the goalie like most players his age. Ten meters from goal he raised his head and he shot the ball into the corner with his left foot.

Boom.

The spectators in the stands cheered. Even the parents of the opposing team cheered for him. The small blond kid had magic in his feet, and they loved it.

"Who is that boy?" a woman asked another person. "He's fantastic."

"He's great," agreed the other man who knew Antoine. "So small, but so talented."

The second goal came just a minute before the final whistle. The Beginners won a corner kick. The ball landed in the box and one small foot pushed it in. 2-1!

It was Antoine again. He did a victory lap and the entire team joined him with hugs and high-fives.

The coaches smiled and nodded.

"Looks like he's ready," Bruno said to David, who nodded in approval. It was unusual because he was still underage, but they knew it was the right decision.

It wasn't long after that Antoine was certified by the French Football Federation, despite being underage. He was always the first to show up for training and the last to leave. He scored tons of goals, but what coaches and teammates loved most about him was his attitude. He never boasted. He would rather pass a ball to a friend in a better position than think about himself. He was mature when it came down to team play.

A year later, Antoine became the leader of the legendary 1991 Macon generation. It was one of the best youth teams of the club. With Antoine, Martin, Jean-Baptiste, and other talented kids, the team began to compete in regional tournaments and brought home a lot of trophies.

"I heard kids say you are the best player on the team," Theo told his brother. They were driving home from another tournament win.

"No," Antoine said. "We have a lot of good players. That's why we win."

Alain listened to the boys' conversation. He loved the fact that his son didn't brag. He just loved to play. He loved to be a teammate.

The 1991-generation team won almost all of their games. But Antoine remembered one game in particular. It was an indoor tournament. They were tied and, in the end, it went into a penalty shootout. Antoine was the last to kick.

All eyes were on him.

He looked at the nervous goalkeeper.

I can do this. Easy.

He kicked the ball. The keeper didn't move. He didn't have to. The ball careened off the left goalpost. Antoine had missed!

Now, it was the other team's last kick. This time, it went in.

Antoine couldn't believe his eyes. His heart sank, and he felt his eyes fill with tears. He couldn't bear that everyone stared at him. He ran out into the parking lot.

Coach David came out looking for him. He touched the boy's shoulder. "Don't blame yourself," he said in a soft voice. "It happens to the best of players."

"But because of me, we lost the tournament," Antoine blurted with a trembling voice.

"No, it wasn't because of you. When we win, it's the team and when we lose, it's the team. Now go in there and get your second-place medal."

"No," Antoine said. "I don't deserve it. I don't like being in second place." He turned his back on his coach and ran down the street. He cried all the way home.

CHAPTER 4

The Anthem

Antoine was seven years old in 1998 when the World Cup took up all of his attention. It was a wonderful opportunity to learn about a great many countries around the world, with amazing players, and everyone arriving in France, who hosted the world's largest tournament! Antoine knew all the French national team players' names and numbers. He loved singing the national anthem with the players and the crowds before the games. Friends came to his home for watch parties and the excitement was high. His mom said that every time France scored, the roof blew off an inch. Everyone hoped that France would finally win the most coveted soccer trophy in the world.

France beat South Africa 3-0 in the opening game. Next was an easy 4-0 win over Saudi Arabia. The next game was scheduled on June 24 in nearby Lyon, against Denmark.

Jean-Baptiste met him at Wednesday's practice, excited. His dad had told him that the French national team, nicknamed *Les Bleus*, was coming to a neighboring town the next day to train before the game against Denmark.

"Let's go and meet them," Antoine said, excited.

"How?" Jean-Baptiste asked.

"Hey, don't worry! We'll figure it out!"

They checked with Alain who confirmed that the French national team was arriving the next afternoon at the central train station.

"Wow!" Antoine said excitedly. "Can we go see them, papa?" he begged.

"Sure, why not?" Alain said. "I want to see them too!"

The next day, Alain drove the boys to the train station. Antoine wore his Zidane jersey and Jean-Baptiste wore a Petit jersey. A crowd of about a hundred fans and a few TV crews were already there, anxiously awaiting the team.

"Here comes the train!" Alain said, his eyes on the timetable board.

The fast train from Paris glided onto the platform with a quiet hiss. The French national team players began to come out after all the other passengers had left. "I see them," someone yelled. People clapped and cheered.

"Where are they?" Antoine said. He was too small to see through the crowd.

"I don't know," Jean-Baptiste said.

Alain wanted to lift his son up, but he was too late.

"Let's go!" Antoine yelled. He began to run into the crowd. Jean-Baptiste ran after him.

"Where are you going?" Alain yelled.

The two friends snuck through the gathering fans and quickly made their way to the platform.

A TV crew was in the middle of filming the event when two blond kids burst into the frame.

"Look at the little ones!" said the cinematographer. "Cute kids!"

It had been Antoine's idea to bring a poster of the French team with them. When Antoine and Jean-Baptiste emerged in the front row of fans, his eyes grew wide. He saw Lilian Thuram and Didier Deschamps speaking with reporters. There was someone behind them. It was one of the best players in the word, Zinedine Zidane.

"Mr. Zizou!" Antoine yelled Zidane's nickname. He jumped in front of his idol and Jean-Baptiste followed. Antoine clung to his poster, his heart beating fast, and opened it wide. "Zizou, can you please give me an autograph?" he asked.

Zidane smiled at the two blond kids and signed.

"Thank you, sir," Jean-Baptiste said. "One more thing?"

Zidane grinned. "What?"

"Please win the World Cup!"

"We'll do our best, kids," Zidane laughed.

"I want to play for France," Antoine said.

"And one day you might," Zidane said. "When I was your age, this is what I wanted, too."

Next, they jumped on Thuram who had just finished his short interview. He couldn't resist the two young fans. Alain saw from afar how the kids were working hard to get their autographs. He couldn't help but smile. Ten minutes later, the two came back, happy and cheerful.

"Look what we got, Dad," Antoine said. "We got all the stars to sign for us."

Jean-Baptiste and Antoine made it on the evening news. Sort of. You could see them in the background, collecting autographs from the French players.

A couple of days later they watched France play Denmark. Each team scored a penalty, but in the 52nd minute, Emmanuel Petit scored into Schmeichel's net and France won 2-1, finished first in the group, and advanced to the knockout stage.

Sunday, July 12, 1998, was a special day.

"The final," Antoine said the minute he woke up. He had hardly been able to sleep, and couldn't wait, so he ran out and hit his ball against the blue door for a good two hours. The Griezmanns, like so many in France and around the world, were seated on the sofa in front of the TV. The World Cup final between France and Brazil was about to begin at the Stade de France, in Saint-Denis, Paris.

It was an exciting month for seven-year-old Antoine. The French team was winning all the way to the finals. He was proud to be French and wore a blue Zidane jersey. He sat excited on the sofa with Theo and Maud, waiting for the game to begin.

"Ronaldo is playing," his dad said with a hint of disappointment to his voice. There were rumors the Brazilian star wasn't fit for the game. But, forty-five minutes before the start, he was added to the lineup.

"We'll beat them, Dad," Antoine said. "We are better."

"Brazil has won the World Cup four times," Alain said.

"And France?" Theo asked.

"Never," his dad said.

"Today we'll win," Antoine said.

As the game progressed, the tension in the room was high and Antoine could hardly breathe. Ronaldo created the first open chance for Brazil in the 22nd minute, dribbling past defender Thuram before sending a cross out on the left side that goalkeeper Fabien Barthez barely diverted. He was one of Antoine's heroes. The best goalkeeper in the world at the time.

But he almost conceded a goal.

In the 27th minute, there was a corner kick for France. "I love set pieces," said Alain and Antoine knew why. The ball went to Zidane's head and, with a perfect header, he drove it into the net.

1 -0 France!

The house exploded in cheers.

Antoine ran to the balcony and screamed, "GOALLL!" It was a scream of joy that erupted from many homes in the neighborhood, as if the entire city celebrated in unison.

The Brazilians attacked again and again. It was already one minute of extra time before halftime and there was another corner kick. Again, Zidane came higher than anyone on the Brazilian defense and scored his second goal of the match. There was another celebration at the Griezmann's household and greater hopes the team could keep the score until the final whistle.

But in the 68th minute, Marcel Desailly got a second yellow card and was sent off. France was left with ten players. The Brazilians felt that they had a golden opportunity to change the course of the game and take the lead.

They attacked the French goal and Barthez fought like a lion to keep his net clean.

Antoine was tense. "You know," his dad said in a calming voice, "Brazil needs two goals, so they send everyone on attack. Then what happens?"

"What?" Theo asked.

"Their defense is loose," Alain said. "All we need is a fast-break counterattack and we score another one."

And he was right.

In stoppage time, substitute Patrick Vieira served a long pass to Emmanuel Petit who scored the third goal for France!

There was a roar from every home in Macon. It seemed that it came from everywhere in France. It was pure joy. On TV, Antoine saw people crying and dancing. And soon they were dancing in the streets of Macon.

France had won their first World Cup ever.

That night, after they'd been celebrating in the center of the city, Antoine went to bed wearing his Zidane jersey. He was exhausted and happy. His mom kissed him, said, "Goodnight sweetie," and tucked him in.

"I want to play for France," he told her. "In the World Cup. And win!"

"Wouldn't that be nice," his mom smiled.

"I think I can do it," he said.

"I think so, too," she said, but he was already asleep.

In the coming week, he asked his friends to sing the French anthem *La Marseillaise* every day before their pickup games. Everyone agreed.

CHAPTER 5

Looking For A Team

The phone rang at Stephane Rivera's house. His mom picked it up. Isabelle, Antoine's mother, was calling. "Where are the boys?" she asked.

"They just got out of the pool," Stephane's mom said. "And they went outside with a ball. Antoine, Stephane, JB, and Martin."

"No homework today?" Isabelle sighed.

"First soccer, then homework," the other woman said. "They are great kids. Antoine is really nice," she said laughing. "He calls me 'Granny.' I'm not that old, you know."

Isabelle laughed. "Everyone tells me that he's a comedian," she said.

"And I love his hairstyle," Stephane's mom said.

"He makes it look like Pavel Nedved," Isabelle said. Stephane's mom knew all about Nedved. He was the brilliant Czech midfielder who played for Juventus.

"You're right, he looks exactly like him with all that blond hair," Stephane's mom said.

"I think he thinks he is Nedved," Isabelle said.

Stephane's dad was the president of the football club. Alain was a coach. The adults spent a lot of time playing, coaching, and attending games and tournaments together. The mothers, too, shared their love of the game.

At the time of this conversation, Stephane, Jean-Baptiste – also known as JB, Martin, and Antoine were all busy doing their goal celebration competition. They'd watched pro players do their dances, and these were part of the game for them. That was because, whenever they played, spending many hours on the pitches all over town, they imagined themselves playing real games. And whenever they scored a goal, they always heard a sea of fans screaming and cheering.

On one summer day, they walked through the neighborhood between buildings, each separated from the next by a vast shiny green lawn. It was hot, and all the sprinklers were on so, when the boys saw the sprinklers, they counted to three and then ran for the grass, sliding on their knees, barely missing the sprinklers as they oozed cold, cascading water.

"What a blast!" Antoine screamed.

They laughed and looked for another set of sprinklers.

Soon, all the sprinklers in the neighborhood were going off in full force.

"What do you think you are you doing!?" a man yelled after them from his balcony when he saw them gliding across the grass in front of his building.

"Winning the World Cup!" JB screamed.

"I know who you are! You are the little Griezmann," the man yelled pointing at Antoine. "And I'm going to talk to your dad!"

"No, I'm not Griezmann!" Antoine yelled back. "I'm David Beckham!"

"Let's go!" Antoine shouted and ran off.

"Hey!" Jean-Baptiste shouted after him. "I'm not afraid!"

"Me neither!" Antoine shouted back. "But there's a pickup game on the next street over!"

Jean-Batiste looked at the other guys and they all charged after Antoine, running at full speed.

They arrived at the game, soaking wet.

That night, Alain came to talk to his son. "Another tryout," Alain said and shrugged. He tried hard not to show how frustrated and tired he was. He knew he had to be strong and confident.

Both Isabelle and Alain looked at Antoine, waiting for a response, but Antoine had just scored a goal in FIFA on his beloved PlayStation. He cheered himself.

But then his eyes met his dad's. He hated the word tryout and hearing it again was like a punch in the gut. He had already gone through five tryouts in the last year and failed all of them. Olympic Lyon, Saint Etienne, Auxerre, Sochaux, and Metz.

He looked at his parents, trying to hide his feelings. "Where?"

"We are going to the CREPS," his dad said. "You, Jean-Baptiste, and Stevie. You'll have fun this time, being there together."

Antoine thought about it. "Okay. Yea!" he shouted. Having his best friends around him made him feel better. He knew that the CREPS was the French Football Federation training center for young players age thirteen and fourteen. If you were selected for the program, you had a good chance of winding up on a pro team someday. It was worth a shot. Antoine knew it was important.

"I'll do whatever it takes," he told his parents. "I know I'm small, but this time I'm going to make it. I will play so good, that no one will care that I'm not as tall or as strong as the other guys." He smiled, and his mom hugged him.

"I'm proud of you," she said.

His dad managed a smile. He was tired of the rejection, too. But his son's words and attitude encouraged him. He knew being a pro footballer was his son's greatest passion, and he also knew that Antoine would never give up without a fight. He also knew one more thing about his son: Antoine was special. Of course, many parents think that about their kids. But Alain was also a coach. He saw talented kids all his life. Deep in his heart, he knew that Antoine had a spark in him. And he had the talent and the character.

Alain was upset that people didn't see what he saw in his son. And sometimes when he lay in bed, he wondered if those coaches and managers and club owners would ever discover what he already knew. That Antoine was destined for greatness.

The following weekend, Alain drove the three friends to Vichy, which was just sixty kilometers away. They knew that if they made the tryout, they would join the prestigious program for the next two years. But none of them really cared. They were three good friends, all thirteen years of age, who were going to play some soccer over the weekend, all under the watchful eyes of professional soccer coaches.

When they arrived at the facilities, it was raining. Antoine loved playing in the rain, and he thought he played very well in the short tryout games, but then came the endurances tests.

They had to run a short distance. The kids lined up for the run. As soon as he started to run, he knew he wasn't doing well. The course was muddy. His legs felt soft and heavy. He came in last.

The second he crossed the finish line he knew it was over. He saw the coach click the stopwatch.

"What happened?" Alain asked, trying to hide his disappointment.

"I was tired," Antoine answered. "I couldn't move fast enough."

His dad nodded. *Maybe we ask too much of him?* he wondered.

So many tryouts. Too many practices. Not enough games. Rejections. They all played a role.

Not surprisingly, Antoine didn't make the team. It was humiliating because it happened in the first round. Antoine and Jean-Baptiste were heading home, empty-handed. Stevie stayed. He made it to the next round. The three boys hugged each other while Stevie comforted his friends and said, "I won't last here long either. I'll join you guys soon." Like Antoine, he had also experienced many rejections.

A day later Stevie, reached the final round and almost made it.

Almost.

CHAPTER 6

The Little Blond Kid

Eric Olhats yawned, jet-lagged. He had just come back to Paris from a trip to Argentina. He was eager to go back to his home in Bayonne, in the Basque Country region of southwest France. But something changed his mind. He wasn't sure what it was. Perhaps it was luck. Perhaps the instincts of a veteran scout who was always on the lookout. Olhats worked for the Spanish club Real Sociedad. He decided that instead of going home he'd stay in Paris and head to the international under-14 tournament in Saint-Germain-en-Laye.

It proved to be one of the most important decisions of his life.

When he took the taxi to the tournament grounds, he still wasn't sure it was the right decision. On the other hand, how could he skip an opportunity to find a gem? Well, truth be told, there weren't many gems around. On most days, he had to sit and watch lots of boring games and go home empty-handed. That was the downside of his job. And it had been some time since he had seen *real* talent.

Half a day had gone by. He was bored and was making his way to grab a coffee when he saw the little blonde kid playing on one of the pitches. There was something that caught his attention. He stopped and watched the game. It was clear to him that the kid didn't belong to the team. He was wearing different socks, so he gathered that the kid was on a tryout. He liked his technical skills and the way he found spaces. He watched the boy intently. The blond kid wasn't strong and was hammered by the opposing players, time and again, oftentimes falling flat on the grass. But he had raw talent. He moved with ease and fluidity. What he did was something you can't teach. You were born with it. Pure talent.

He began thinking that going to the tournament hadn't been a waste of time after all.

"Who's the little blond kid?" he asked a man who sat near him, cheering.

"My son's best friend," the man said proudly. "They are playing for Montpellier, but they are actually from Macon. They are here for a tryout."

"I see," said Eric. "And who's your son?"

"The center forward," said Stevie's dad proudly.

"He's good," Eric said. "And I'm surprised he's in a tryout. Both kids play as if they have played for Montpellier for a long time."

He introduced himself. "I'm a scout. This is what I do for a living. And your son is very promising."

Stevie's father couldn't look more pleased. He gave Eric the names of the two players, Stevie and Antoine, and Eric handed him his business card. "You'll hear from me," he said. The beaming father told him later everything he wanted to know about the kids. They were so good, he mused, but all they had faced so far was one rejection after another.

"I bet they say Antoine is too small," Eric said with a wry smile.

"That's exactly what they say!" said Stevie's dad.

Eric chuckled. People were always looking for athletic players. Fast and agile. But the kid was only thirteen. And he believed that, when he grew up, he would compensate with his technical ability and his game vision. Eric was confident the kid would toughen up. What he liked most about the boy was his attitude. He seemed keen on making himself useful everywhere on the pitch. He had game intelligence. That was a winning combination.

When the match ended, Eric saw the blond kid walk up to the stands with a pack of biscuits. Eric went to the bar, bought another pack, and came back. He sat near the boy. He opened his pack and munched on one of the biscuits.

"You like it here?" he asked.

"Yes. I love playing," Antoine answered, looking at the man. He was stocky with full-dark hair and a beard.

"I'm Eric," the man said. "And you?"

"Antoine."

"You want to trade biscuits?" Eric asked. "Yours look great."

It was a strange thing to ask, Antoine thought, but the guy looked friendly.

"I'll give you one of mine," Antoine said smiling. "But keep yours."

Later, Eric went back to the bar and, while drinking coffee, he recalled a conversation he'd had a few months ago with a Montpellier scout who had visited him at Real Sociedad. The scout had told him about the young Griezmann. This might be the kid I just saw, he thought.

He decided he wouldn't go home. He'd stay at the tournament for another day and watch all of Montpellier's games.

But he was interested in only one player:

The blond kid. Antoine Griezmann.

CHAPTER 7

The Note

Stephen Blondeau, the under-13 Montpellier coach, took a break. His team was doing okay but not great, and they were set to play PSG in the afternoon. He was tired and longed for a nice break to eat his lunch by himself in the tournament cafeteria. But his plans were interrupted by the man who took a seat opposite and gave him a big smile.

"Team is doing great, I see," the man said.

"Thank you," said the coach.

"The kids are well-coached," the man went on. The coach looked at him and wondered what he really was up to. "I saw this blond kid," the man said, "and I thought – wow – the kid is very promising."

"Who? Griezmann?" asked the coach. "I have better players than him. He isn't actually our player. We brought him here for a tryout."

The other man shrugged. He introduced himself as Eric Olhats from Real Sociedad. He shifted the conversation to how challenging it was to coach young players. Stephen was more open to talking about that because Eric was friendly and knew a thing or two about the sport. They finished the conversation with a handshake and Blondeau rushed to his team while Eric Olhats made another mental note:

Montpellier isn't interested in young Antoine Griezmann.

Now he had to finish his plan. The tournament was winding down. He already knew from their conversation that Stevie's dad was driving his son and Antoine back home. He knew he should approach Antoine's dad first, but he wasn't around. So, Eric decided to bypass the coach, who didn't seem interested in Antoine, and to connect with the boy himself. It was a delicate matter because you weren't supposed to get in touch directly with a young player. So, he found a way around it.

Antoine wiped the sweat off his forehead and trotted off the pitch. They'd come in twelfth place, but he didn't mind. He didn't know if the coach wanted him back and he decided not to think too much about it because he didn't want to be disappointed. *I'm going home*, he thought. Although his parents were on vacation in Croatia, he wanted to be in his room with his PlayStation or outside with the blue door. And he was missing his friends.

Then someone blocked his way.

"Antoine?"

"Yes," he said. It was the man who had offered him a biscuit.

"Eric," the man introduced himself again. "I have a note for your parents." He looked around as if he didn't want anyone to watch, pulled a folded piece of paper from his pocket, and handed it to Antoine. On the front, it read: "To be opened only when you get home."

Antoine took the paper and slipped it into his pocket. Eric nodded in approval, said, "See you later," and disappeared.

Antoine went in to change his uniform. In the locker room, he touched the paper. Wondering what was on it was driving him crazy. Finally, he took it out. He had to know what the note said, but he waited until he was in Stevie's dad's car and on their way home. More relaxed as they drove, he took out the note and unfolded it carefully.

"Dear Mr. Griezmann," the note read. "My name is Eric Olhats. I'm a scout for the Spanish club Real Sociedad. I saw Antoine play in the tournament, and I would like to invite him to a week-long tryout with our club. All travel costs and accommodations will be paid by us. Please call me at your earliest convenience." A phone number was scribbled at the bottom.

Antoine couldn't breathe for a moment.

"What is it?" Stevie asked.

"A guy came up to me and gave me a note for my dad. He invited me to a Real Sociedad tryout."

"Oh, that guy," said Stevie's dad while he was busy steering the car onto the highway. "I told him who you are. He said he wants to invite Stevie as well."

"That's awesome!" Stevie beamed. "The two of us are going to Spain!"

"Not so fast," Stevie's dad said. "We need to talk to the guy some more."

The two boys were happy. Antoine didn't think the Montpelier coach was so hot on recruiting him, so the offer from Eric was flattering. He wondered how his parents would react. When he got home, he unfolded the note and stuck it on the refrigerator door. The next day when his parents arrived, his dad saw it.

"What is this?" Alain asked, and Antoine told him the entire story.

"So, a stranger who claims he works for Sociedad approached you and offered you a trial?" his dad asked.

"Yes, he did," Antoine said. "He seemed like a nice guy."

"Okay," Alaine said. "I'll discuss it with your mom and see how she feels about it. But to tell you the truth, I'm sick and tired running around to all these tryouts where nobody seems to see your potential. All I hear is how frail you are and how slow you are, and they never seem to see how good you are. So, now we go again to Spain and what will happen there?"

"I want to do it," Antoine said. "Please let me do it."

At dinner, his mom had the same reaction. "You are only thirteen and a half," she said. "If they'll take you, you'll be away from home, in another country. It won't be easy for me, your father, or your brother and sister; and it will be very difficult for you."

"But Mom, I want to be a professional player, and this man really wants me. No one in France wants me. It's a chance of a lifetime," Antoine reasoned. "And also, I won't be alone. They want Stevie, too."

"You talk as if it's a done deal. It's only a tryout," Alain reminded him. "I'm a bit burned out. After so many rejections we might as well take a break and try again next year."

Antoine looked at the note Olhats had given him and said. "Dad, why won't you call the guy and see for yourself?"

Alain studied his son for a moment, then nodded. He picked up the phone and began talking with the scout. When he hung up, he said, "Okay. He's coming to Macon on Monday. We'll meet and see what his intentions are."

Antoine was dancing with joy in the living room.

"Thank you, Papa!" he said and kissed his dad. "You are the best!"

CHAPTER 8

A New Home

Sprawling along the banks of the Rivers Adour and Nive, the waterside city of Bayonne, the capital of the French Basque Country, is one of the prettiest in southwest France. Bayonne's colorful medieval buildings and the cobbled streets by the river came into view when the car driven by Eric Olhats made its way to his home. In the passenger seat sat a 14-year-old boy from Macon, only 5'1 tall. What he did not have in stature, he made up for in excitement. His dream of becoming a pro player had begun earlier that day when his parents drove him to Lyon airport. Eric had picked him up and, while they cruised to Eric's home, he told Antoine how things were going to unfold.

"You are going to stay with me, at my home for about two to three months," he said.

"And then?" Antoine asked.

"And then, we'll see," Eric said.

Antoine knew his contract with Real was for only three months, after which the two sides could terminate or continue for a full year. By the end of the year, the club would decide if they wanted to keep him. With a salary. But for now, they'd pay his expenses, tuition, and a couple of flight tickets home. Eric knew that staying with him would make the transition period smoother for Antoine. The boy came from a close-knit family. He was surrounded by friends he'd grown up with, in a city and neighborhood he knew well. Here, he had to learn to speak Spanish and get used to a different culture. He would have to study and train with kids, teachers, and coaches he didn't know. The hardest challenge, though, was the absence of Mom, Dad, and his brother and sister. The club had decided not to recruit Stevie, Antoine's friend. It would have been much easier for both of them to be together, so Eric felt it was his duty to make Antoine feel at home.

I'll be there for him, Eric thought.

Antoine enrolled in a program that enabled him to study and graduate from Eric's home. "Studying by yourself isn't easy. You'll have to be very disciplined. I know that your grades aren't great, but your schooling is important," Eric said.

Antoine smiled. His teachers back home were always telling him that he should try harder at school. One of his teachers had told him, "I know that you think that you don't have to work hard in school because you'll end up being a soccer player but, if things don't go your way, you'll be better off graduating with good grades in order to succeed in life and find a job." Antoine didn't care much about it, because it never occurred to him that he wouldn't end up a pro soccer player.

Eric knew what Antoine was thinking. "You are smart," he said, "But a good education will make you a much better player." Antoine wasn't sure what Eric meant.

"Being a professional isn't only about playing on the pitch. It's also about what you do when you are off the pitch," Eric explained, although he knew that it would take some time for Antoine to understand fully what he meant.

"No PlayStation until you are done with school stuff," Eric continued. "Whenever you need help, just ask and I'll help. As for your soccer routine, five days a week, I'll drive you to evening practices in Zubieta, Real Sociedad's training ground. Each practice starts at 6:30 and ends at 8:30. Then I'll pick you up and drive you home. We'll get here at around 10 pm, so be prepared for long and busy days."

"How far is Zubieta?" Antoine asked.

"About 35 miles from here. It's in San Sebastian."

They approached Eric's house. He brought the car to a halt and shut off the engine. He helped Antoine with his suitcase and opened the door wide.

"Welcome home," he announced. He entered and Antoine followed. Eric climbed the stairs and showed Antoine his room.

"You like it?"

"Yes, very much. Thank you." Antoine was impressed but felt a bit strange. He sat on the bed for a moment. Eric opened the curtain. The sun streamed in and Antoine thought it made the room more pleasant.

"Hungry?" Eric asked. "I'm starving."

"Me too," Antoine said.

"I'll make us something to eat," Eric said. While he was working in the kitchen, Antoine kept asking him questions. The boy was tired but still very excited.

At night, when he was in bed, Eric came by his room.

"It was a long day," he said. "You look very tired."

"I am," said Antoine. His eyes shone.

"Did you speak to your parents?"

"Yes." Antoine's voice trembled. "I told them I was fine."

Eric looked at him. He knew that the boy was already homesick.

"Good," he said. "Tomorrow we have a very busy day, so you have to get a good night's sleep."

"Okay. I think I'm gonna be fine."

"I'm sure you will," Eric smiled, although he had his doubts.

Five minutes later, Antoine was sound asleep.

CHAPTER 9

The Training Grounds

E veryone on the U-14 team at the Zubieta training center noticed the new kid. He was small and blond. And he made sure he smiled when he approached his teammates. One-by-one, he shook their hands. Luki Iriarte, the coach, smiled when he saw the look on Antoine's face. No one does that here, he thought. A kid with manners. Imagine that. He already liked him.

The Zubieta training center was the pride of soccer in the area with seven training pitches scattered about a beautiful and broad hillock. Antoine loved it the moment he arrived on the first day. He didn't get why some of the kids thought it was weird when he shook their hands. He realized most of them didn't speak French. Why would they? This was the Basque Country and people spoke Euskera, the Basque language, and Castilian, a flavor of Spanish spoken in northern and central Spain. Still, he was in high spirits. He had heard there were a couple of French players in the academy. And one of the coaches — Julen — spoke French. No more time to think about different languages and customs and stuff. Training began and everyone on the pitch spoke the international language of soccer.

When Antoine touched the ball for the first time, he passed a defender on the wing and made an incredible pass into the box that ended with the center forward scoring. Coach Luki smiled again. This time broader. He liked his players to be quick and aggressive. He wanted them to be aware of what spaces were available once they have the ball at their feet. If they can do that and make quick decisions, they can grow into great players. Griezmann was fragile, small, and skinny. But he was talented. He knew what to do a half a second before the other players. As the first practice progressed, the coach knew he had a promising player on his squad.

When the practice ended, he went over to Antoine to talk and asked Julen to translate.

"Keep doing what you are doing. You'll work hard, and our system will make you a much better player."

Eric was waiting for Antoine outside. It was almost nine o'clock in the evening.

"How'd it go today?" he asked when Antoine got in the car.

"I'm not sure. I didn't understand a word. But I liked the practice," Antoine said.

Eric started the car and grinned.

"It's a start!"

When they got home, Antoine was exhausted, but he wanted to talk to his parents before he went to sleep. When he heard his dad's voice, his eyes welled up with tears.

"I had my first practice today," he told his dad.

"And you were your usual brilliant self?"

Antoine chuckled. "Well, I thought so, but it's different from how we train in France," he said. "And most of the time I have no idea what they're saying. But the coach told me he liked me. He said I have to get stronger and faster, but he wasn't worried about it. He said he would work to make my game more physical. He liked my skills."

"It sounds great," Alain said. "I know it must be tough for you."

"It's worth it, Dad," Antoine said. "It's what I've always wanted."

"We know, son," Alain replied. "Take care."

"I will." He paused, then said, "I miss you guys."

Alain heard his son's voice tremble and he felt a knot in his stomach.

"We miss you too." Alain saw Isabelle looking at him and knew how much she wanted to talk to

Antoine. "Mom wants to talk to you," he said. "We are here for you. Call us whenever you like."

Antoine's mom picked up the phone and asked if he was eating well. He told her that the food was good, and he liked being with Eric. "He takes care of me really well."

"That's good to hear. Do you have friends?" she asked.

"No, not yet. No one understands French..." his voice trembled again.

Isabelle took a deep breath. She knew he was about to cry.

"In a week, everyone will be asking to be your friend," she consoled her son. She wanted to add, "... and you can come back home wherever you want," but she decided it was too early for that.

"I'm okay, Mom," he said. He didn't want her to feel bad, so he pretended to be okay. "Don't worry. I'm doing fine. Can I speak with Theo and Maud?"

"Yes." She sent him kisses and hugs with a heavy heart. It was only a week since he'd been gone, but she missed him badly. She knew he missed them, too, and it broke her heart.

"Don't worry, we'll be together real soon," she told her son, then handed the phone to her daughter. "He's already homesick," she whispered to Alain.

Alain nodded. He had his own doubts. If Real wound up signing Antoine, he would be away from home for a few years. Just thinking about it made him shudder.

Did we make the right decision? he thought. *Only time will tell.*

Antoine talked to his little sister and then to Theo. He had no problem with Maud, but he couldn't hide his real feelings from his brother. "I'm thinking about you guys all the time. Our home. My room."

"I miss you too, brother," Theo said. "I know you had to do it. But it's hard."

Antoine felt the knot in his throat. "I'll come visit soon."

"How's your game?"

"It's hard. I'm not sure I fit to tell you the truth."

"If you don't, you can always come home," Theo said.

"Yeah, I know."

Antoine hung up. Eric offered him cookies at the kitchen table. When Antoine sat opposite him, he saw the redness in Antoine's face. He knew he had been crying.

"I have some good news for you, Antoine," he said cheerfully. "You are not going to be living alone in this house with me. You're going to have a roommate. A kid your age."

"Really?" Antoine looked at him surprised.

"Another kid joined the academy and is coming to stay with us."

"Spanish?" Antoine asked.

Eric grinned. "No. French."

Antoine brightened up instantly. "That's fantastic!" he said.

"Goalkeeper," Eric said. "A really nice kid. I know his dad."

"But anyway, in three months I'll have to move to the dorms," Antoine said.

"Maybe, maybe not. We haven't decided yet," Eric said. "I'm more than happy to have you here. You can stay here as long as you want."

Antoine's eyes widened with surprise. "Thanks, Eric." He stood up and hugged his host. "I really appreciate it."

Eric knew that if Antoine moved to the dorms, he'd be running back home to Macon the next day. He had already talked to the club management about prolonging Antoine's stay with him and they'd agreed. He thought about what coach Luki had told him the other day:

"Antoine has a special touch. He can invent a dribble that could win a game. His first touch is exquisite. And one more thing: when I saw Antoine Griezmann touch the ball the first time, the sun came up."

It was glowing praise. Eric decided not to tell Antoine what coach Luki had said yet. He knew he had to do everything to keep Antoine in the program. The kid could become a great player. He wouldn't let him drop out. He'd be there for him until everyone saw what he and Luki saw in Antoine Griezmann.

A star in the making.

CHAPTER 10

A Friend at Home

E ric was true to his word. A few days later, he brought home the new kid from the train station.

"Antoine, this is Alex. Alex Ruiz, the newest member of our little family," Eric said. Antoine greeted Alex, shook his hand and showed him the house.

"Where are you from, Alex?" Antoine asked.

"Pau. From the French Pyrenees," Alex exclaimed with a broad grin. "It's about an hour's drive from here. I wanted to stay with Eric because I didn't like the idea of staying at the dorms."

"Great!" Antoine said. "It's ten times better than the dorms. Eric told me you are a goalie."

"Yes," Alex said. "You?"

"I play behind the forwards usually, but not here. When they put me in, I play on the wing most of the time. I'm not scoring as much as I used to back home. I love to create chances for the attack. But I see the bench a lot."

"I wonder why?" Alex asked.

"They say I'm too small." Antoine sighed. "And they have their own way of teaching the game. The Spanish way. It's different from what I am used to, and I guess I am a slow learner." He smiled.

"My dad said that the first year is always tough," Alex said. "I got into the Olympic Lyon academy. But I left."

"Why?" Antoine asked.

"I was happy when they recruited me, but it was too far from home. I got homesick bad. I begged my parents to put me someplace closer to home. Now I can see my folks every week."

Antoine felt a pinch of envy in his gut. If only Olympic Lyon had accepted him, he would have been closer to home.

"How did you wind up here?" Alex asked. "Why aren't you playing in France?"

"Real wanted me," Antoine said. "And I wanted them." He didn't want to tell his new friend that all the French teams had passed on him. It was still too painful to think about it.

"Real Sociedad is a great club," Alex said.

"Yes," Antoine said. "It's cool that you came here to live with us. We'll have fun together. It's especially cool that I can speak French with you."

"You don't know Spanish?"

"Not very well."

Alex flashed a smile. "I'll teach you."

Alex gave Antoine a lot of hope and he was happy to have a friend in the house but, at least once a day, he had a moment when his mood darkened. He thought a lot about his family and friends and how unhappy he was being relegated so often to the bench. Coach Luki must have thought he wasn't making enough progress. Antoine hated sitting on the bench and although Eric's pep talks always helped, they never lasted long. When night fell and he was all alone in his bed, he was miserable. He wanted to call it quits many times. But then morning came and he got so busy he forgot all about it.

One Saturday afternoon, the U-14s played another local team. Xabi Alonso played for the guests. Antoine's team was leading 1-0 when Luki asked Antoine to warm up. He came on in the 60th minute. They only had two subs because a lot of the kids were injured. The other team's coach, Miguel Gonzalez, looked at the blond kid who ran onto the pitch.

"Who's that?" he asked his assistant.

"Antoine," the assistant looked at the team's roster sheet.

"Antoine what?"

"It only says 'Antoine.' No last name."

"Well, he's good," said Gonzalez after a few minutes. "He's small and weak but he creates great chances. His passing is superb."

Gonzales was still talking to his assistant when Antoine got the ball on the left side of the pitch near the box and, with his left foot, crossed a beautiful pass to his forward who didn't flinch and hit the ball hard. The finish was immaculate, and the ball went in. 2-0 to Real U-14. The forward hugged the small boy with the long blond hair, blue eyes, and pointy nose. Antoine smiled and made a little dance, and everyone laughed.

"Brilliant pass," Gonzalez said to his assistant. He looked at Luki who was smiling and gave him a nod. Luki was impressed but was wondering if Antoine would make it in their system. Something was missing. The puzzle named Antoine Griezmann was a work in progress. Still, he meant what he'd said about him to Eric. He wouldn't give up.

CHAPTER 11

Home and Away

As more time passed, Antoine called his parents less and less. They always heard the pain in his voice, and he didn't want them to know how unhappy he was. So, he started texting them or leaving voice messages.

He went home three times a year. During the holiday season, in February, and for summer vacation. Real paid for all three trips home. Going home was a blast. He loved it. His old friends were all there and it was fun playing together and hanging out in the city he loved so much. And he was surrounded by his family, which made everything right. But then, there always came the last day. Saying goodbye with a heavy heart and putting on a smile, while the tears choked his throat.

Alain drove him to the airport. Isabelle stayed behind. It was too hard for her. No one talked the whole way. Antoine sat in the back, doubled-up. He cried softly, and his dad just drove and didn't say a word. But after a while, he couldn't stand it anymore. He had to say something.

"Antoine," Alain said, "you are a free agent. You can come back home if you want."

Antoine thought about it. He appreciated that. "No," he said. "I'm going to do this. I'll show them."

Later that year, the entire family made the trip to San Sebastian for the big tournament. They spent time at Zubieta, sitting in the stands, waiting for their son to play. But the coaches benched him one game after another. At the end of the tournament, Alain and Eric had a conversation. Eric took one look at Alain's face and knew he was upset.

"These past four days were horrible," Alain said. "We came to see our son play, and then we find out the coach doesn't think he's qualified to play. Not even for a single minute. This is unacceptable. I think we made a big mistake letting him come here. You came to us a year ago. You convinced us to send Antoine here. For what? To sit on a bench? Why keep this charade going another minute? If he isn't destined to become a pro, we might as well bring him home. I sent you a happy child and now when I look at my son's face, I want to scream."

"I understand how you feel," Eric said. "You are his father but let me tell you something. I feel the same way. Antoine's like a son to me, too." He spoke softly. "Don't give up, Alain. Give it another year. Trust me."

Alain looked at Eric. He wasn't sure. "I believe in him," Eric said. "He'll make it. I know he will."

But as the year wound down, nothing changed. Eric tried to figure it out. What was missing? Another tournament was approaching. Eric knew that if Antoine blew this one, it would all be over.

Eric decided to do something.

"Antoine, wake up," Eric whispered.

"What? What happened?" Antoine opened his eyes. He saw Eric's face close by. His kind eyes. A light from the corridor cast his shadow on the wall.

"Out of bed," Eric said.

"What time is it?" Antoine yawned.

"Midnight. You've been asleep for two hours."

"What happened?" Antoine looked at his host dumbfounded.

"Get dressed. Wash your face. I want to show you something."

Antoine nodded and yawned again. "Okay. Give me five minutes."

They left the house and although Antoine was totally puzzled by what was going on, he decided not to ask questions. They went to Eric's van and drove for five minutes. He stopped the car next to an old warehouse with a big wall.

"Let's get out," Eric said.

"Why here?"

"You'll see." He took a bunch of balls from the back. "We're going to do some training."

It was a dark night. Eric turned on the van headlights and the wall was instantly flooded with bright light.

"We are going to play balls against the wall," Eric said. "I'm going to smack the balls on the wall. You have to intercept and pass them to me. Got it?"

"Yes," Antoine said, still half-asleep. "I have a little experience with this."

It reminded him of his blue door at home, the door he'd spent hours hitting balls against. It all began there. His love for the game. And now here he was again, in front of a wall, and this time they want him to play against it.

Eric started with one ball, and then a second and a third. He hit the wall with a rain of balls, and Antoine passed them back to him or took control of them. He couldn't deal with all the bouncing balls, but Eric didn't stop. He was yelling his instructions.

"Move faster! Before the ball hits back! You're too slow! Faster! FASTER!"

Antoine didn't mind taking direction. It was fun. There was something special that night. As the practice went on, he got faster and more accurate. They took a break. "You always have to get to the ball first. You need to ask for it. You have to be there to get it first and to pass it," Eric said. "With your skills, you'll keep it and you'll have the edge. You'll make the right pass. You'll score."

They did it for an hour. Suddenly the car lights died. They stopped in their tracks, engulfed in darkness.

"Uh-oh," Antoine muttered.

Eric looked at his car. "The battery's dead," he said.

"Wow. Do we have to stay here all night?" Antoine joked. He was in a good mood.

"No, no," Eric said. He called a friend he knew was always awake until late and asked him to come out and jumpstart the car.

"He'll be here in ten minutes," he said. "Practice is over. Let's drink some water and head home for a good night's sleep."

CHAPTER 12

The Turning Point

*T**hree Years Later.*

"I like this kid," said Meho Kodro to his assistant, Inigo Cortes. The two men from Real Sociedad had watched Antoine train for a month in the 2008-9 season.

"He's opened up," said Cortes and Meho agreed. When they'd first met him, the 16-year-old had been shy and only hung around with two French-speaking friends, Jonathan and Lucas. But, as the season progressed, everyone on the team discovered how fun and mischievous he was.

After practice, the two coaches asked him to come over to their office for a talk. Antoine stepped in cautiously and sat down next to Inigo, across the desk from Meho. They spoke in Spanish.

"We are happy to see you making progress," Meho started. He saw that Antoine was nervous, chewing his lower lip. The boy smiled.

"Thank you, sir," he said.

"Everyone on the team likes you," Meho said. "This is very important to us. But there is still is a lot of work to do. I think that Inigo and I agree that you are very good technically and you have some great skills and game intelligence, but you aren't strong or fast enough yet."

Antoine had heard this so many times he didn't even flinch.

"But we can improve this and bring you up to speed. Every Tuesday and Wednesday after training we are going to work with you individually."

"We call it a weakness session," Inigo interjected. "We'll focus on your pace and strength."

"When do we start?" Antoine asked.

"Well, Inigo," Meho said with a smile. "What day it is?"

"Tuesday," his assistant said.

Meho leaned forward across the desk. "Right now."

The three went out of the office and onto the pitch. Antoine was tired. It was already 9 pm. Usually, by this time he was already on his way home. But not tonight. They made him run. They made him jump. They made him lift weights. Two serious coaches who believed he had a great future and wanted him to excel. Antoine responded with hard work. After an hour, he could hardly breathe. His legs were heavy. His muscles ached. He looked at the two men with pleading eyes.

"Ready to quit?"

Breathing hard, Antoine nodded enthusiastically.

Meho smiled. "Ten more minutes!"

Antoine nodded. It was the longest ten minutes of his life.

When Antoine woke up on Good Friday morning, 2009, he was ready. Today was special because the squad was having their first group game in the international youth tournament. Outside, he heard rain coming down and he jumped out of bed, hoping they would not cancel the game. In his heart, he had a good feeling about today. He felt like it was his time to shine.

He came down and found that his roommate, Alex, was already there with Eric, eating breakfast.

"Good morning Antoine, ready for the big day?" Eric smiled.

"I am," Antoine said. He joined them and ate with a big appetite. When they were finished eating and cleaning up, Eric drove them to Zubieta. Alex was the team's first goalkeeper. He knew he would wear the keeper's shirt every game. Antoine hoped he'd be able to start. In the weeks before the tournament, he'd stayed late every Tuesday and Wednesday for the one-on-one training. Coach Meho had told him what he thought about him. "You are intuitive and read the game better than anyone. And now, because you have worked so hard on your athleticism, you are performing better than ever. You can score. Create opportunities for your teammates. But when you have the opportunity, strike. You have a great left foot. Use it."

Real Sociedad's international youth tournament was established in 1985. The best youth teams in the world participated each year and, over the years, it became a launching pad for some of the biggest names in the sport. But in 2009, the tournament was made up of Spanish clubs only. Real was in the group stage with Athletic Bilbao, Sevilla, and Barcelona. In their first game, Real faced its archrival from Bilbao, another great Basque team.

Antoine stopped breathing in the changing room when Meho Kodro announced the starting lineup. When his name was called, he felt overjoyed. He wanted to jump up, hug his coaches and teammates, and dance. But he held back. He didn't want to jinx the opportunity. He would save the celebrating for when there was something celebrate about.

From the first whistle to the last, he knew he was in his element. Years of working hard had brought him to this moment. He was active on the pitch, fought for every ball. And he knew it was coming. He scored his first goal in the 31st minute. When he saw the ball land inside the net, he ran along the pitch, waving, with a bright smile on his face. His teammates piled on him. He was so happy he wanted to embrace the cheering fans. When the match ended, his coach told him, "This is your first. You're going to score many more," and he was right. He scored four more goals in the group stage and led his team to the top of the group, ahead of Barça.

They were in the final against Atletico Madrid. The game was played in Real Sociedad's stadium, the famous Anoeta. They led 1-0 most of the game but, in the 82nd minute, the ref whistled for a penalty and Atletico equalized. At the end of the game, the two teams got ready for a penalty shootout.

Everyone looked to Alex, the goalie.

"You are going to bring us the trophy," Antoine told him with a smile. He tried to hide his emotions. He was as nervous as everyone else. They were better than Atletico and they deserved a win. But he knew that penalty shootouts are like a lottery. A little luck always helps. And sometimes, the lesser team wins.

Alex nodded.

The two teams started the shootout with two good shots. Then came the third. Alex would remember this shot always. He saw the player's face. He saw how nervous he was. You can tell by the way a player goes to the white mark. You can see the hesitation in his face. And Alex knew that the shot would go to the left. The whistle was heard and the entire Anoeta crowd stopped breathing. The shot went to the left and Alex dove and stopped it. The ball bounced, and everyone erupted in cheers. The next shot was theirs. They didn't miss it.

Real won the tournament.

It was Antoine's best day since he'd come to the Basque Country. Three and a half years of struggle ended right there on that field. When he lifted the trophy and the crowd exploded with cheers, he felt jubilant. He was the tournament's top scorer with five goals. He danced in the changing room with his teammates. He sang and laughed and hugged everyone. In his heart, he knew that he had made it.

A month later he signed his first contract with Real Sociedad. It would go until 2014 and, with the blessing of Loren, the team director of football, he was promoted to the reserve team.

There was no turning back.

CHAPTER 13

The Substitute

M artin Lasarte saw the gloomy faces in the Real Sociedad's president's office. He'd arrived in San Sebastian from Montevideo, Uruguay, as the new manager of the team. He was tired from the long flight, but he knew what was expected of him.

"As you know, Martin," the president told him, "two years have passed since we were relegated from La Liga to the second division. The fans are unhappy. We almost made it back last season. But almost isn't enough."

"I know why you brought me here," Lasarte said. "I am also aware that the club doesn't have a lot of money to buy big-name players."

"So, what is your plan?" asked the president.

"I'll dig into the academy. Players that you worked hard to develop. There are always great gems who want an opportunity. A chance to shine."

The president smiled. He liked the new coach's attitude. Usually, new coaches wanted big budgets to sign up players, but Martin didn't ask for that and he had already proven his ability to find great young players. He'd discovered and nurtured an 18-year-old kid named Luis Suárez in Nacional and launched the storied career of the Uruguayan national.

When the meeting was over along with handshakes and smiles, Lasarte prepared for his first pre-season friendly. He wanted a 22-player roster. He wanted to see at least two players in each position. Everything was fine until, two days before the friendly, something happened that changed his and Antoine Griezmann's lives.

Antoine fought hard for the ball with his U-19 teammate, Bingen. The two players tried to intercept a high ball and Antoine crashed into Bingen's back. Bingen fell onto the grass.

"I'm sorry!" Antoine said. His teammate twitched his face in pain. "It's my back," he said to the team physician. He was immediately escorted to the changing room for further treatment.

The next day, coach Lasarte heard the news from his assistant. "Bingen," the assistant said, "the player we planned to have in the left-wing, is injured."

Lasarte couldn't believe his luck. He sighed. "So, find me a substitute. I want a left-footed winger. Like Bingen."

"We don't have one on the reserve team," said the assistant.

"Then bring me one from the academy," Lasarte said.

The assistant thought for a moment and said, "Let me talk to their coaches. I think there is someone who might fit. I have to warn you – he's kind of young. But clever."

"Can he score with his left?"

The assistant smiled. "Yes."

"Bring him on," Lasarte said.

When word came down from the first team that Lasarte wanted him in practice to fill Bingen's spot, Antoine felt bad for Bingen.

"It's not your fault," Eric told him. "You need to grab this opportunity with both legs." He was excited. Coming off the U-19 into the first team and bypassing the reserve was too good to be true. He knew that Antoine wouldn't disappoint the new manager. *It's a chance of a lifetime*, he thought, but he didn't want to put pressure on Antoine, so he kept his thoughts to himself.

Antoine didn't give it much thought. He believed that, after the friendly, he'd return to the U-19, or to the reserve if he was lucky.

When Lasarte first saw Antoine on the training grounds, he wasn't sure. "He's small," he said to his assistant.

"Yes, but he has great qualities," his assistant said. "Besides, he's the only left-footed midfielder we have."

"Okay." Lasarte waved to Antoine and Antoine trotted over.

"I heard you have a great left foot," the coach said.

"My right isn't bad either," said Antoine with a smile. Lasarte smiled back. The kid didn't look nervous. In fact, he had a whimsical gaze in his blue eyes and looked more like a high school student than a pro footballer.

"Good," said the coach. "You'll get your chance to show what you are made of."

On August 1st, 2009, Antoine was in the 22-player lineup for his first game with the pro team. They played CD Anaitasuna from the sixth division in front of eight hundred spectators. At the beginning of the second half, the entire squad on the pitch was replaced. When Antoine Griezmann trotted onto the pitch, it began to rain. He closed his eyes for a second and made a little prayer.

His first goal ever for the first team came in the 69th minute. The goalkeeper bounced the ball. Antoine jumped in, intercepted it and shot the ball with his left into the net. He scored one more from outside the penalty area in the 81st minute. This one was a volley that made the coaching staff gasp.

Later that night he called his parents. "They interviewed me on TV," he said trying to control his excitement.

"That's incredible," Isabelle said, trying not to cry.

"What did you say?" Alain asked. He was proud of his son but felt frustrated he couldn't be there with him and, to make things worse, it hadn't been broadcast on French TV.

"I told him I was happy I scored in my first game."

"Twice!" Isabelle said.

"Yes," Antoine chuckled. "And then one of the journalists told me he thought I was ready to play for the first team and I told him I was only eighteen so I have a long way to go."

"Good answer," his dad clapped. "You have to be modest. Did you see yourself on TV?"

"Yes," Antoine said. "It was embarrassing. But hey, I did the entire interview in Spanish. I hope I didn't sound silly."

"Never!" his mom exclaimed.

"What happened later was even better. In the changing room," Antoine said, "the manager and I had a talk."

"What did he say?" Alain asked.

Antoine grinned. "He wants me on the first team for the rest of the pre-season."

There was a moment of silence at the other end of the line before the entire Griezmann family erupted in cheers. Antoine listened to his parents tell the news to his brother and sister. He could hear them cheering in the living room and he was overcome with joy. He wanted to be there with them, badly. But he knew there was much work to be done.

Antoine scored two goals in the next game and became a sensation overnight in the local media. Everyone wanted to talk to him. Everybody wanted to talk about him. The French kid from Macon became a local celebrity.

"I don't like this media circus," said Lasarte to Imanol Idiakez, the coach of the reserve team. "I don't want it to go to his head."

They invited Antoine for a meeting before practice to make sure he was on the same page.

"You are doing great," said Lasarte. "But after only two games, the media is already going crazy. They are flattering you and making you the hero of the moment."

"You talk as if there's something wrong with that," Antoine replied.

"There's nothing wrong, but it's not real. The first time you have a bad day, they'll come after you – and we don't want that, do we?"

"No," Antoine said. He'd already had the same conversation with Eric at home. "I don't care what they write about me. I only care about getting better as a player and helping the team."

"I just don't want you to burn out," said Imanol. "You are my player. A reserve player."

"I know," Antoine said. "Thank you so much for the opportunity. I know that being on the first team is temporary."

When he left the room Martin Lasarte said, "I like the kid. He has great qualities."

"I agree," said Imanol.

"We need to be very careful with him," said Lasarte. "I'm going to ask Diego Rivas to look after him." Rivas, who had come to Real from Atletico Madrid, was thirty years old. Lasarte wanted him to be Antoine's mentor and an older brother figure. Like everyone on the team, he liked the talented French kid who was friendly and fun and, at the same time, very shy around the first team players.

"I want you to look after the kid," Lasarte said to Rivas.

"I will, coach. Don't worry," Rivas answered.

CHAPTER 14

One Day I'll Be Like Them

Rivas woke up with a start in his hotel room in Tenerife. He glanced at his watch and realized he had been napping for a good two hours. It was five o'clock in the afternoon. He wondered where his roommate was and figured the kid was probably taking a walk. He got out of bed and threw open the balcony curtains. The sun was blistering hot outside. He saw Antoine's bare back; he had his headphones on and was moving to the music. Rivas went out and touched the kid's shoulder. Antoine turned his head and smiled. His face was as red as a lobster.

"What are you doing out here in the sun?" Rivas said. "It's hot as hell."

"You were asleep, and I didn't want to wake you up," Antoine said with a shy smile.

"But look at you!" Rivas gushed. "You are completely burned. It's going to hurt you later!" They went inside.

"Sorry, I...," Antoine said. "... I didn't know it was going to get this bad."

"Oh man, I told Martin I'd look out for you. He's gonna kill me. I have to get some lotion on you or you won't be able to play tomorrow!" he said, digging a bottle of lotion out of his bag.

Antoine took the bottle of lotion and spread on his sunburned body. "Thanks, Diego, appreciate it. Any longer and you could put a fork in me."

Antoine didn't play in the tournament. His team won while he sat it out on the bench. But that didn't last long. A couple of weeks later, they played against Eibar. When he kicked the ball with his left from outside the box, the ball came off his shoe like it was shot from a cannon and the desperate goalkeeper dove helplessly as it slammed into the back of the net. That was a reminder to everyone that Antoine Griezmann was becoming a monster scorer.

"You are doing really well," Lasarte told Antoine. "I'm happy with your progress."

"Thank you, boss," Antoine said.

"I'm going to put you on the roster for our 100th-anniversary game at the Anoeta against Real Madrid. You earned your place, Antoine."

Antoine tried hard not to jump and scream. He just smiled and said, "That sounds great, boss."

On August 15, 2009, with the Anoeta full to the brim with excited fans, they played Real Madrid who came to town loaded with a roster of stars and superstars. Before Antoine came on in the 61st minute, the home team had surrendered two goals scored by Sneijder and Benzema.

Lasarte tapped his back. "Play your usual game," he said. Lasarte knew the kid was nervous to play against Cristiano Ronaldo, Benzema, Raul, Kaka, and company but he hoped he would face his fears once he was on the pitch.

When he trotted in, Antoine saw Rivas, giving him a supporting thumbs up. They'd had a conversation in the changing room. "The game will be very physical. Let the big guys take care of that. Just enjoy the game. If you're relaxed, you're going to deliver. Play it as if you are at practice," Rivas had told him.

Antoine took his position. Everywhere he looked, there was a big star. The biggest names in the game.

He took a deep breath. One day I'll be one of them, he thought.

His eyes met Ronaldo's. He smiled, and Ronaldo smiled back.

But this wasn't a smiling contest. After some running around, he finally got the ball. He controlled it, dribbled along the wing and made a perfect pass to Rivas who was running inside the box. The fans cheered wildly but Rivas missed his shot. He looked at Antoine and nodded in approval. From that moment on, Antoine played his regular game. He wanted to score and to win in front of the home crowd but it wasn't meant to be. They lost 2-0. Lasarte told him after the game that he'd been great. Antoine thanked him and thought, this is my last game with the first team. I'm back to the reserve.

The new season was fast approaching. Lasarte was still missing a strong left-footed winger. "I'm trying to bring Jeffrén Suárez from Barça," Loren, the director of football, told him.

"That's what you said last week," Lasarte said, frustrated.

"Barça is playing a game," Loren replied. He was also frustrated.

"I have a Plan B," said Lasarte.

"What's that?"

"Antoine Griezmann," said Lasarte.

"But he's just a kid," Loren said. "He needs at least another year in the reserve to be ready."

"He's great," said Lasarte. "I think he fell down from heaven. That's how special I think he is. He scored five goals in the pre-season. He can play on the wings. He plays behind the striker, makes great assists, and scores. Amazing left foot and a good right foot. His passing is immaculate. Free kicks.

Corner kicks. And on top of all that – he's smart. A fast learner. And if Suárez stays in Barça, you'll get a player that cost you nothing. A player you developed in your own academy. Seems like a no-brainer to me."

"I know he's done well for you but I'm just not sure he'll perform on the first team, Martin," Loren said. "Tell you what. If we don't get someone else for this position by the end of the week, it's your call. Bring in your boy. Put him on the roster."

Lasarte nodded. He knew that the burden of the proof would be on him. He was betting on an 18-year-old kid who had just stepped out of the academy. But his gut told him that he was doing the right thing. He believed that Antoine would prove himself invaluable in Real Sociedad's quest to return to La Liga.

Chapter 15

Number 27

By the 73rd minute, it was time. A few minutes earlier, Lasarte had told Antoine to warm up. He was grateful because he'd thought that this moment would never arrive. He'd sat on the bench for most of the team's first league game. And he was worried he'd stay there for the second game, too. He pulled on his training shirt and was checked by the fourth assistant referee who nodded and raised the board with Antoine's number.

There were fans in the stadium who wondered who number 27 was. But when they saw the small blonde kid waiting anxiously on the line, they clapped and cheered.

A couple of days earlier, when Lasarte had told him that he was included on the first team, Antoine was asked what number he wanted on his shirt. "Give me any number with a seven in it," Antoine told his coach. He knew that the jersey with the seven on the back was taken by Franck Songo'o, the midfielder from Cameroon.

His family and his childhood friends smiled when he'd told them about his number choice. They knew why Antoine liked this number so much. It was Beckham's number and Antoine had adored Beckham since he was a young kid in Macon. He'd had posters of Becks in his room and he loved his style: a playmaker, a passer, a master of the free kicks, and a great scorer. Plus, David Beckham was cool. He wasn't just a footballer. He was an international celebrity and a trendsetter.

Jonathan Estrada came out. Antoine hugged him and trotted in. He was eighteen years, five months and sixteen days old when he debuted. Although the game ended in a scoreless draw, the supporters were very happy with the new addition to the team.

Later that night, he called his family and told them about the game. Everyone was excited. He didn't tell them that Lasarte had hinted that he might be a starter. Apparently, Estrada who was the left-winger wasn't doing well, and the coach made it clear that he'd begun to lose trust in him.

On a gray September day in the Anoeta, Antoine was in the starting eleven for the first time. He was happy and ready. He wanted to do something great in the game against Huesca. He'd always dreamed about his first goal in a league match. This was it. This was the day.

He was confident, but the first thirty minutes of the game were frustrating. He told himself not to get lost. He had a tendency to disappear sometimes. He had to make his mark. He worked hard on the line, running back and forth, trying to create good passes and find the empty spaces. And then he got a perfect pass from Aranburu about 18 meters from goal. He dribbled and hit the ball hard into midair with his right foot. The keeper couldn't save it. The ball landed in the back of the net.

"Antoine Griezmann scores his first goal in a league game. And with his weak foot!" exclaimed the TV commentator.

When Antoine saw the ball deep in the net, his lungs pumping, the fans cheering, he ran toward the stands and kissed the team logo on his shirt. The fans went wild. He was the happiest man in the world.

At home, they watched the game on the internet. Everyone cheered. In the changing room after the celebration and after he was interviewed by a sea of journalists, he saw a message from his mom.

"You made us all proud. I wish we could be there with you now. We love you."

"Thank you, Mom. I love you too. I wanted all of you to be here. This is the greatest day of my life." He choked with emotion

He couldn't sleep, and he thought about the goal all night. He didn't think about the future, but there were more to come. More goals, more wins, and many dreams that would come true. And as time passed, there was no doubt in anyone's mind that a star was born or that Antoine deserved his place in the roster.

It was Real's third year in the second division. The mood in town was gloomy. The fans talked only about one thing. Could they make it to La Liga?

Little by little, the fans began to believe it might happen. The team was at the top of the table and they were playing very well under Lasarte. Antoine was focused on each game, but he was also interested in lifting the mood of the fans. They are too serious, he thought. And he decided he would bring some fun to the Anoeta.

He thought about his after-goal celebrations. This was an opportunity to show his fun side. His creative side. Not just running or diving and raising his fist to the sky. He would come up with something that would make everyone happy. He got his chance in a freezing winter game against Cadiz. They were leading comfortably, 3-1, at the 90th minute when the fourth official showed three more minutes to go. Antoine took over the ball in midfield and made a run from the right side of the pitch into the box and slammed the ball above the keeper's head into the net. He knew it was time to show off. At the edge of his eye, he saw a pile of snow that hadn't been cleared from the sideline. He ran in and dove on top of the snow. *Big mistake.* It was freezing and as hard as a rock. The minute he hit it, he felt the pain in his knees. He smiled to the fans, who went crazy, trying not to show how hurt he was.

"That looked like it hurt," his Uruguayan teammate Carlos Bueno said, hugging him.

"Yes," Antoine grimaced. "That was stupid."

Bueno smiled. "And they say I'm crazy."

They both laughed. The ref ended the game and the crowd clapped enthusiastically. It was Antoine's fifth goal of the season. The fans loved him, and they started to believe that they were witnessing a special season.

Carlos Bueno became Antoine's new mentor. He was a talented striker who'd played for Sporting Lisbon and PSG before moving to Real on loan.

One day after practice, Antoine saw Carlos walking back to the pitch.

"Aren't you going home?" he asked him.

"No. I have still work to do," Carlos said. "Training after training is the most important thing you can do."

"Can I join you?" Antoine asked.

"Absolutely."

"What are we practicing today?"

"How size doesn't matter," Carlos answered. "You see, you and I aren't tall. But still, we should work on headers. Because, as a footballer, you have to be able to do everything. So how does a player like us still score with a great header?"

Antoine shrugged. "I don't know. How?"

"We jump higher," Bueno laughed. "But there are some things we can do to improve the way we intercept the ball. And once we have it, it's all about how we find the net."

They began working. Just the two of them. Every evening after practice. Antoine found out that Carlos was right. Carlos taught him to get the right timing to jump. And, when he was in midair, to stay there a second longer and to work with his body to control the header.

They worked on free kicks and how to position themselves better in the box. Carlos was a scorer. And Antoine wanted to improve his scoring. And every night he learned something new from his mentor.

Coach Lasarte wasn't crazy about what they were doing – he thought that they needed rest after the regular practice, but the two insisted and he caved in.

On June 13, 2010, Real beat Celta Vigo 2-0 and won the second division title. The first goal was a penalty by Prieto that was given because Antoine was fouled in the box. The second was sweet because it was an assist by Antoine to Carlos who headed in a perfect goal. When Lasarte saw it, he smiled. The after-practice practice was all worth it.

It was a rainy day in San Sebastian, but nobody cared. Players and fans, soaked to the bone, were dancing and cheering. They were back in the best league in the world.

For Antoine Griezmann, it was the most important year of his career. From a complete unknown, he'd become an integral part of the club's biggest achievement in years.

Other teams in Europe were talking about him. So Real offered him a new contract. They wanted their upcoming star to stay home.

It was also time to leave Eric's home and go live in town. He was no longer a kid. Three months with Eric had become almost four years. Eric helped him pack and put his stuff in Antoine's car. They hugged for a long time. Antoine felt the tears welling in his eyes.

"Without you, I would never have made it," Antoine said. "This home will forever be a part of my life."

Even Eric became emotional. Antoine had a great family. A supportive mom and dad. But since the boy had entered his life and lived at his home, he'd treated him like his own son.

Yet, it was time to move on. The shy young boy had become a man. Since he'd met Antoine in the Paris tournament, Eric had always known the kid was special. He'd been right. And it made him happy. This was a once in a lifetime experience, even for a man like him who spent most of his days scouting for the next big player. He knew that one day – not so long from now – Antoine would become one of the world's best.

CHAPTER 16

The Spaniard

The sun was out and bright on the day Antoine's plane touched down in Lyon. It was a beautiful day and, at the terminal, a chauffeur for the French U-19 national team was waiting for him with a sign with his name on it.

He shook hands with the driver and climbed into the car. They made their way to the familiar Olympic Lyon training grounds where the team trained for the U-19 World Cup.

He got emotional as they approached the training grounds. His thoughts drifted to the past, not so many years ago, when he was thirteen. He remembered how his dad had driven him here for Olympic Lyon's academy tryouts. It was the first of many tryouts and Antoine had been excited and happy. After all, he was a fan of OL. Playing for them had always been his dream and the dream might become a reality soon. He'd been sure of it!

He remembered the drive from Macon to Lyon. His dad had been in a good mood. He'd thought that Antoine stood a good chance of making it in the academy because he had received a glowing review from an OL scout, Alain Dutheron, who'd seen Antoine play in Macon. The scout had been impressed by Antoine's extraordinary skills. He'd written in his notes: *This kid is a joy to watch. He can see one step ahead of everyone. He made a difference in every game I saw him play in.*

But he'd also noted that his parents weren't tall. Which meant that young Antoine wouldn't be tall when he grew up. That was an issue because the French academies were looking for tall, athletic players. Still, he'd been so impressed with the kid, that he recommended that his directors at the club recruit Antoine for a limited time. Watch him play. Monitor his progress and then make a decision.

Antoine had been happy. He'd thought he was doing fine in the first tryout. The coaches had told him to come back for weekly training for the next month or so because they wanted to observe him more closely. Father and son drove to Lyon every Wednesday afternoon and, after five weeks, they'd had a phone call. "We would like to meet you in Macon and see if we can sign something."

"They want me, right?" Antoine had asked his dad.

"It seems that way," Alain had said. "But we have to hear what they offer first."

Antoine had nodded and smiled. He'd been sure he had been accepted. They were coming to Macon to meet his parents. They had to be serious. He was confident.

Alain and Isabelle had attended the meeting at the UF Macon clubhouse with Alain Dutheron who'd come all the way to Macon with his colleague Gerard Bonneau. Serge Rivera, the club president, was also in attendance. The parties had shaken hands and sat down for small talk. Everyone had been in a good mood until it was time to get down to business.

"We liked Antoine very much," Dutheron had said. "He's a talented kid. We think that he has a bright future. But at this moment in time, we have a very good group of kids who we really want to play, and we don't have enough spots open for the year."

Alain had exchanged looks with Isabelle. They hadn't expected this.

"Are you saying you don't want him?" Isabelle had asked. Alain could tell her heart was heavy.

"We want him, Madame Griezmann," Dutheron had said. "We came here to make an offer."

"Which is?" Alain had asked with a knot in his throat.

"We are willing to sign him up now, but he wouldn't join the academy until next year," the scout had said.

The room had fallen silent. Alain had looked straight into the scout's eyes.

"No thanks," Alain had said. He hadn't had to think too hard – it was humiliating. He had been to training. He had seen the other kids. He knew he wasn't objective but, still, he thought Antoine was one of the best.

The two men from Olympic Lyon had looked at each other. They'd been sure the Griezmanns would accept their offer.

"I don't understand," Dutheron had said. "Why?"

"Because you want us to wait a year," Alain had explained. "A lot of things can happen in a year. In the meantime, we plan on exploring more options, and next year, if you still want my son to join your program, give us a call and we'll let you know."

Alain Griezmann had been determined. The meeting was over. The visitors had shaken hands with Alain and Isabelle and left. Antoine's parents had walked home in silence and seen their son waiting outside with a ball in his hands. His eyes had shone with excitement when his parents arrived home.

"Did you sign?" he'd asked with a big smile. But then he'd seen the look on their gloomy faces and understood immediately that something was wrong. And his heart had sunk.

"We couldn't accept their offer," Alain had said, studying his son's face. Isabelle had hugged Antoine. She knew how disappointed he was.

"But why? They came all the way to sign me!" Antoine had whispered.

"Let's go inside and I'll explain," Alain had said.

They'd sat at the kitchen table, and Antoine had listened to his father intently with tears in his eyes. He'd been sure that by the following week he would be wearing an OL jersey. He had been dreaming about it his entire life. He would grow up to become their star and, later, the French national team star. That is how he'd pictured it. And now he had to wait a full year to realize his dream.

Alain had been as disappointed as his son. He'd exchanged looks with Isabelle who was caressing Antoine's back. As a matter of fact, she'd also been taken by surprise when Alain had turned down Olympic Lyon's offer.

"I know how upsetting this is. I'm also upset and angry myself," his dad had said. "But I didn't want to waste a year. There are other teams. Good clubs out there that will recognize how good you are and sign you up."

Antoine had thought about it and wiped away the tears with his hands.

"What if no one wants me? Can I still go to OL next year?"

"Of course," his dad had said. He hadn't wanted to tell his son he wasn't so sure. A year is a long time. Lots of things change in a year.

And Alain Griezmann had been wrong about the other clubs. During the 2004-5 season, not one team in France wanted to sign Antoine Griezmann. Saint Etienne, Auxerre, Sochaux, Metz, Montpellier, and the French youth program – all said no to Antoine. Later, Alain had doubts. Maybe he had done the wrong thing. Maybe he should have accepted the OL offer. It was better than nothing.

And then Eric Olhats had stopped by the Paris tournament, saw Antoine, and knew at once that the little blond kid was special. No one in France had seen his potential, so Antoine went to a foreign country to fulfill his dream, away from his family and friends. All by himself, struggling and fighting and never giving up.

The car came to a halt. Antoine got out. He could see the French U-19s warming up on the pitch. It was a perfect day to start his career in France. He wasn't bitter. He was happy for the opportunity. Now, five years after they'd rejected him, he came back as a rising star in Spain, and French football coaches were paying attention to him. They didn't know much about Antoine Griezmann, but they knew they couldn't overlook him anymore.

They called him "The Spaniard."

But not for long.

CHAPTER 17

Oh, my Grizou!

"I want him on my team," said Didier Deschamps when he watched Antoine play for Real Sociedad and the French U-21 team. He saw the potential.

In 2014, Antoine was Sociedad's star in La Liga. There were strong rumors about a possible move to Atletico Madrid that angered the fans. It was no secret that great clubs around Europe were knocking on his door.

But back in his homeland, he was still an unknown to most people. They would ask: "Antoine who?" when his name was mentioned. But Deschamps always thought about the long haul. He'd been nominated as France's national team coach in 2012 after a disastrous period that had seen the French squad collapse in the group stage of the 2010 World Cup in South Africa. The French were beaten out and sent packing, but that was only part of the story. A players' mutiny against the French federation and a fight between the coach and the players had destroyed the team and left the fans disinterested and disappointed.

It was the worst period in the French national team's history and Deschamps, who was a key player in winning the World Cup trophy with the French team in 1998, was tasked with rebuilding the team and restoring its pride.

He began working with two big tournaments in mind – the 2014 World Cup in Brazil and the 2016 European championship that France was hosting. His game plan was to build a team that would be a mix of veterans and new faces. He liked Antoine's versatile style, playing behind the strikers, on the wings, and helping the defense. Antoine always wanted to do more and aspire to become a better player but, most of all, he was a team player. *The kid loves his job and loves football and that's why he gives so much on the pitch and in training*, Deschamps thought. *He's always smiling, he's good-humored, and he is good with everyone on the team whether they are older or younger.*

On 13 May 2014, Antoine was named to Deschamps' squad for the 2014 World Cup. He scored three goals in the friendlies leading to the World Cup and was chosen for the starting eleven in France's first World Cup game in Brazil, where he replaced the injured Franck Ribery on the left side of *Les Bleus'* attack as they defeated Honduras 3-0.

The French team was doing well until they met Germany in the quarter-finals and lost 1-0. That was the moment when all of France discovered the kid from Macon. This wasn't the humiliation of 2010. France lost, but the fans saw a motivated and well-trained French team. Everyone knew the stars of the team. But who was this blond kid who was crying after the game ended? The cameras zoomed in on him. He was genuinely hurt. Everyone at home and around the world felt his pain. Who was this player who came from nowhere, who nobody knew? The one who cared about the team. The one who cared about the fans. The one who cared about his country.

They were moved.

Overnight, everyone in France knew his name. They started to notice what a good player he was. They fell in love with his smile, with his funny and creative celebrations after he scored. And they started to believe that this kid and a bunch of young motivated players could lift France back to the top of world soccer.

Deschamps was right. In the next four years, The Spaniard became a major player on the team, a beloved household name in France, and one of the top players in the world.

Antoine was playing Fortnite in his hotel room the day before the 2018 World Cup finals in Moscow, Russia. He was drinking *Mate*, the Yerba tea his Uruguayan friends loved to drink. Since his early days, his Real Sociedad days, he had made friends with Uruguayan players who taught him about soccer and life. Coach Martin Lasarte, who had promoted him straight out of the academy to the first team, had taught him to accept his shortcomings. His mentor, Carlos Bueno, had taught him to love the way they played in South America. He admired how they gave everything for their team, never gave up, and always helped their teammates. When Uruguay qualified for the World Cup, Griezmann had welcomed the team players at the airport with a *Mate* in his hand, wearing the official Uruguayan shirt.

He hadn't wanted to meet Uruguay in the World Cup, but he was ready. First, before entering the field, he had hugged all the Uruguayan players one-by-one in the tunnel. But later, when he scored, he didn't celebrate. His teammates ran to hug him, but he remained quiet.

His phone rang. It was his best friend, Atletico teammate and Uruguay's captain, Diego Godin. "Everyone in Uruguay is talking about you," Godin said. "People are devastated by our loss, but they admire how you behaved on the pitch after scoring."

Godin talked about the finals. "I think you can make it," he said. They talked about Croatia and then Godin wished Antoine luck. "I'd love to see you lift that trophy tonight my friend," he said.

Deschamps told his players, all the way to the finals, not to lose focus. "It's only seven games," he repeated. "You enter the pitch and you don't give an inch. You fight all the time. Every second. Seven games and you become world champions."

France showed the world a team with lots of talent and passion. Antoine was part of a great front made of Olivier Giroud, Blaise Matuidi, and Kylian Mbappe. He scored three goals and assisted two, earning him the nickname 'Grizou' – a moniker inspired by 'Zizou', as Zidane is known.

Deschamps called him 'my Grizou.'

Antoine thought it was too early to be likened to Zinedine Zidane. He felt he hadn't earned it yet. Maybe later tonight, after the game.

Since that morning, he had been playing a game plan in his mind. He thought like a coach. Always. Not only what he'd do but also how his teammates would play. He thought that France's defense was vital to winning the game. He talked about it in the changing room with his teammates. They loved his ideas. They listened.

France has conceded four goals in six games en route to the final, three of which had been scored by Argentina in a thrilling 4-3 victory in the quarter-finals. Antoine said to them, "The defense, for us, is the most important thing, because we know that, at the front, we can score a goal at any time, either with Kylian on the overlap, with Olivier in the center, or with me in a little madness that can happen to me once in a while." He smiled and added, "We are proud to be French. We have a beautiful country; we have a great team and I want people to feel proud of being French."

The phone rang. One of the assistant coaches reminded him that in 30 minutes he should meet with the team in the lobby before going to Luzhniki Stadium for a short practice.

In his heart, he knew they would win. He couldn't explain it. That's why he felt calm and confident.

A lot had happened since he'd joined the team. He had evolved as a person and a player. He got married to his girlfriend, Erika, the year before. They'd met when he played for Real Sociedad and they had a two-year-old baby named Mia, who was godfathered by Diego Godin. His entire family was in town for the duration of the World Cup. He thought about the two finals he hadn't won – the European championship in 2016 where France lost to Portugal in the final on home soil, and the Champions League finals playing for Atletico against Real Madrid where he'd hit a penalty into the crossbar. The tied game had ended in a penalty shootout where he scored but Real won 5-3. In both cases, he remembered looking at the trophy before the game.

He'd decided not to look at the trophy before the 2018 Europa League finals in Lyon against French team Marseille.

Lyon again. The stadium he'd wanted to play in as a kid. The stadium of his childhood dreams.

He'd wanted so much to look at the trophy before the game but resisted the urge. It worked. He'd scored twice and won his first ever big trophy.

The big night arrived. Antoine tried not to cry when he heard the French anthem. This was it. The final. Earlier, the team had been greeted by the French president in the changing room. The mood was jubilant. There was a feeling in the air that they were going all the way. When the game started, his adrenaline was overflowing.

He was happy. Happy to play in the world's most important game. He was happy because he knew he was there to make a difference. He was there to win

And when the referee whistled for a penalty for France in the 38th minute, all eyes were on Antoine.

A billion people watching, all over the world. He was calm. He was focused. He knew he was going to score and he felt, at that moment, that the trophy was a sure thing. He was right.

France won 4-2.

When he'd been a boy, he'd talked to his dad about soccer for hours on end. At home. At the training grounds in Macon. During the endless hours of driving from one tryout to another. At all times. Everywhere. Everywhere but the bath at home in the evening. That time had been reserved for Mom, and she'd talked about everything but soccer. They'd talked about his friends, his school, about life in general. Then one day, they'd bravely let him go. He knew how hard it had been on them. Especially on his mom. It had been hard for him, too. But now, as a grown man and a father himself, he understood completely how they felt. When he saw them in the stands cheering for him, he waved back. And cried. Finally, he let himself look at the trophy. He held it. He kissed it.

Erika brought Mia down to the pitch. He held her in his arms, beaming. In France, the entire nation was celebrating. In Macon, as in every city in France, people chanted his name. The small kid from the neighborhood near the sports center who'd fought against all odds was a world champion.

Deschamps ran toward him and hugged him.

"Oh, my Grizou," he shouted to his player, who had just become the player of the match.

At that moment, Antoine didn't think about the future. He wanted this moment to last forever.

A few days later, in Macon, the city came to the city square to celebrate with their local hero. The entire Griezmann family stood on the city hall balcony. Isabelle, Alain, Theo, Maud, Erika, and little Mia.

Antoine's dad spoke into the mike. He thanked everyone. And then he said, "Antoine, I love you."

He knew his father loved him. But that was the first time he had heard him say it. Antoine looked at his happy family like his mom and dad had looked at him growing up. He saw his childhood friends in the crowd. He saw his coaches. His teachers. And when he closed his eyes, he could see the blue garage door dotted with the marks of soccer balls. The blue door that had been his soccer training ground all those years ago when a little blond kid kicked a ball at it, perfecting his touch. The kid who dared to dream that one day he'd become the champion of the world.

THE WORLDS #1 BEST-SELLING SOCCER SERIES!

THE FLEA

The Amazing Story of Leo **Messi**

Michael Part

Cristiano **Ronaldo**
The Rise of a Winner

Michael Part

Neymar **The Wizard**

Michael Part

Mohamed
The Egyptian King
Salah

Michael Part & Kevin Ashby

Harry
The Hurricane
Kane

Michael Part

Luis **Suarez**
A Striker's Story

Michael Part

James
The Incredible
Number 10

Michael Part

Eden Hazard
The Wonder Boy

Michael Part

Antoine Griezmann
The Kid Who Never Gave Up

Michael Part & Steve Borg

Made in the USA
Monee, IL
14 January 2021

57611469R00069